TRINITY OF COACHING

GOD, YOU, AND YOUR LIFE COACH

A Practical Guide For Creating A
Successful Partnership Through Positive Change

DENEEN K. ATTARD MSM, CBT

ISBN-13: 978-0615856766

Table of Contents

Introduction

Today, people of all ages and professions are seeking assistance from coaches to help them navigate life through today's changing and demanding world. They are looking for someone to help them achieve goals, balance life, restore relationships, create financial security, and find spiritual peace. This book provides information on how to incorporate Christian faith and Biblical principles into everyday life and coaching sessions for both clients and coaches.

This book emphasizes the importance of a partnership between the client, the coach, and the Holy Spirit, who is the ultimate Coach. With this book, you will learn how prayer, positive affirmations, forgiveness, optimism, intentional thinking, and self-discovery can help you uncover your strengths and live a full, rewarding life.

Whether you're a coach or a client of a coach, you will benefit from the principles and insight presented in this manual. If you're a coaching client, this book will help you gain the most from your coaching sessions by using Biblical principles. It is intended to strengthen your relationship with God, yourself, and others. Each chapter is followed by an application section to help you put the information into practice. It is important that you spend time in prayer prior to your coaching sessions and that you implement the action items listed at the close of each chapter.

If you're a life coach, this book will help you incorporate your Christian faith into your coaching sessions. It will also aid you in creating an atmosphere in your sessions for your clients to examine their faith and to grow in their personal walk with God.

Each chapter will also include life applications for you to consider in your role as a coach.

As you learn Biblical principles from this book and apply them to your coaching sessions, I believe you will have better results from your coaching experience. Together with the help of the Holy Spirit, you and your life coach or coaching client can make a wonderful team!

Keys to Success

Keys to Success for Coaches:

- Acknowledge and respect the client's faith
- Avoid preaching to the client
- Avoid leading the client
- Be transparent with your client
- Understand you are on a journey of discovery with your client

Keys to Success for Coaching Clients:

- Acknowledge where you are in life
- Embrace change
- Be transparent with yourself, God, and your coach
- Allow God to lead you
- Forgive yourself and others
- Walk in love with others

"Listen to advice and accept instruction, that you may gain wisdom in the future. Many are the plans in the mind of a man, but it is the purpose of the Lord that will stand."
—Proverbs 19:20-21 (ESV)

"Coaching is a transformational process to redirect behavior and support change."
—Randy Helms

1

Life Coach 101

Did you know working with a life coach can be an empowering experience? Coaching can help you to respond calmly to stress, make choices more easily, and increase creativity–all of which can lead to living a more successful life. Having a life coach can also help you to unlock answers to questions, uncover hidden saboteurs to your success, and create a positive mindset that will allow you to become your best. It is no surprise that people from all occupations seek out the assistance of a coach to help them reach their personal and professional life goals.

Life coaches can help you find greater success in different areas of your life including your relationships, your career, your environment, your hobbies and recreation, your health, your finances, and even your spiritual life. Regardless of which part of your life you wish to work on, you can supercharge your results by incorporating your Christian values and Biblical principles into your coaching sessions. When you do this, you are collaborating with God and inviting Him to do His will in your life. You are also allowing Him to uncover the specific changes you need to make in order to grow both naturally and spiritually. When you acknowledge His authority in your life, you are creating a solid foundation on which He can operate. You are also demonstrating your willingness to commit to His purpose and plan for your life.

If you're a Christian, the coaching experience deepens when

Biblical principles are incorporated into your sessions and when the Holy Spirit is allowed to be your supreme life coach. This Word-based approach enhances the coaching experience as the Holy Spirit guides you through the process. However, this does not mean you can passively go through the sessions under the misconception that your coach and the Holy Spirit will handle everything. Rather, you must actively engage in the process by being transparent and honest in your self-evaluation. You must recognize that you are a work-in-progress, and you must acknowledge your need to improve certain areas of your life.

Finding just the right life coach is very important and something you should not take lightly. When selecting a coach, it's important to consider one whose words, philosophy, and skill set works best for you. Take time to prepare for an interview with a prospective coach by determining what is important to you. Approach the selection process prayerfully, and be open to the Lord's direction and guidance.

As you research your options for a life coach, don't be shy about asking questions. Since a life coach can play a crucial role in your personal success, it's important for you to feel comfortable with your coach, his standards, his beliefs, and his values. Below is a list of questions you might consider asking a potential coach during the interview process:

1. Are you a Christian? If so, what does that mean to you?
2. How are you able to incorporate Biblical principles into our sessions?
3. What governing organization do you adhere to regarding your professional conduct?
4. What can I expect from my sessions?
5. What can I expect from you as a coach?
6. Why did you become a coach?
7. What type of training have you received?

The answers to these questions will reveal the potential life coach's personal beliefs, expectations, and coaching approach.

During your conversation with a life coach, listen attentively and take notes. Ask for clarification if necessary, and make room for transparency in the interview. If you begin the process with open communication, you are less likely to regret your hiring decision later.

Now, let's take a moment to look at the above questions in a little more detail:

Are you a Christian? If so, what does that mean to you? You might feel uncomfortable asking this question, but it's an important one to ask. Even if a coach is advertised as a "Christian life coach," it is wise to seek clarification. Posing this direct question about the coach's personal relationship with Jesus allows the coach to share his views with you and gives you an opportunity to determine if you and the coach are a good match.

Regardless of the answer given, it is important to remember that you are not attacking that coach's faith or religious beliefs. When you ask the potential coach about his spiritual convictions, be sure to speak in a non-confrontational, friendly way. This warm approach will alleviate the potential for the coach to feel threatened by your pointed question. However, if the person does become defensive, refuses to answer the question(s), or has a different view from you, then you will need to consider how this might influence your coaching sessions.

How are you able to incorporate Biblical principles into our sessions? How little or how much you want to incorporate Biblical principles into your session is entirely up to you and should be discussed with the coach during the interview process. If you want to incorporate prayer, scriptures, or other Biblical principles into your session, then discuss it with your coach. If the coach in question already has a specific Christian program he works with, ask him to share some information with you about how the program works.

What governing organization do you adhere to regarding your professional conduct? When working with a life coach, you should know if he is accountable to some governing body. The International Coaching Federation is one of several nationally recognized governing organizations for life coaches. Once you find out what organization a particular coach is under, you can research the organization to discover more about the guidelines and verify the life coach's affiliation.

What can I expect from my sessions? Some life coaches will offer a complimentary session that will allow you to experience the flow of a coaching session. If you are able to take a complimentary session, note the communication dynamic between you and your coach, the overall flow of the session, and the conclusion reached at the end of the session.

Because each session should have a purpose, you should have accomplished a goal or found some form of resolution at the end of the session. Of course, you will not accomplish every goal in each session, but you should have some sense of accomplishment at the close of the session.

Over the course of your coaching sessions, you may experience the following changes or resolutions:

- a shift in your thinking
- a clearer vision of whom God created you to be
- new insight into a situation
- decrease in distractions
- diminished anger
- freedom from toxic relationships
- increased confidence
- improved mental and physical health
- accomplishment of a goal

What can I expect from you as a coach? Your coach is there to support and help you reach your desired goals. He or she is also there to challenge you and hold you accountable to reach your highest potential. However, your coach is not there to do the work for you, nor is he there to make decisions for you. It is also important to remember that coaching is not counseling or therapy, nor should it take the place of psychiatric care.

Why did you become a coach? Hearing the other person's story will allow you to know your coach better and possibly find a connecting point that resonates with you. When you ask this question, listen carefully and feel free to ask follow-up questions that will help you understand the coach better.

What type of training have you received? This question is very important and should not be overlooked. You want to make sure that the coach you select has completed some form of coaching training and is able to provide proof if you desire.

Coach Application: As a coach, your role is to facilitate the client's agenda, not create the agenda.

Client Application: As a client, you are in charge of the agenda and goal setting. Take the necessary steps to ensure that you are prepared for your coaching sessions. Resist the urge to "wing it." Have a goal in mind regarding what you want to achieve while working with your coach.

Reflection: Now that you better understand how to approach the coaching process, what do you hope to gain from your coaching session?

"Give instruction to a wise man, and he will be still wiser; teach a righteous man, and he will increase in learning."
—*Proverbs 9:9 (ESV)*

"A coach is someone who tells you what you don't want to hear, who has you see what you don't want to see, so you can be who you have always known you could be."
—*Tom Landry*

2

Are You Coachable?

Working with a life coach is a serious process that requires a huge supply of your time, energy, finances, and emotions. Before signing on with a coach and committing yourself and your resources to this endeavor, you must first determine if you are coachable. It is better to realize your level of willingness and transparency before engaging in a long-term coaching process.

When determining if working with a coach is right for you, consider asking yourself these key questions before diving headfirst into coaching sessions:

1. *Are you ready for change?*
2. *Are you willing to be an active participant in that change?*
3. *Are you ready to have your beliefs challenged and perhaps your goals redefined?*
4. *Are you committed to the process of coaching?*
5. *Will you speak with honesty and be transparent with your coach and yourself?*
6. *Can you financially afford coaching without incurring debt?*
7. *Are you free from any substances that would hinder your progress?*
8. *Are you able to set aside time daily to work on the coaching process?*

If you answered yes to all of the questions, then you are probably ready to work with a coach. A successful journey with your life coach requires commitment and transparency. The coaching process requires that you, the client, be in the driver's seat regarding setting goals and establishing an agenda. The coach is there only to keep you focused and on track. He or she is not present to "tell" you what to do regarding the situation. Of course, you can ask for feedback from your coach, but the final decision is up to you.

As you evaluate your readiness to commit to the coaching process, prepare yourself to give an honest answer to your coach's questions. During your sessions, your coach will ask some probing questions. He or she will also challenge you to go deeper to uncover any hidden issues. Unlike a regular conversation, your coach may interrupt you during the session to gain clarification or request more information. At first, you may be tempted to resist your coach's questions and approach. However, if you will commit to working through the temporary discomfort, you will gain the desired long-term result of success.

Once you've evaluated your "coachability" and are willing to commit your resources and emotions, you can confidently move towards finding a coach. If you've realized you're not quite ready for a coach, that's okay. You can take this time to reflect and prepare before committing yourself to the coaching process.

Coach Application: Coaching is not necessarily for everyone; therefore, your role is to make sure your clients are coachable and that they understand the commitment necessary to attain the results they desire. For this reason, you will need to implement direct communication to determine their willingness to commit to the coaching process.

Client Application: Be honest with yourself as you explore your decision to work with a coach. Determine if you are able to make the mental and physical commitments required while working with your coach. Make sure you gain a clear understanding of what is expected of you and how your results will be measured.

Reflection: Are you coachable? How do you know? If not, what areas will you need to work on in order to work with a coach? How do you plan on making those changes?

"For God so loved the world, that he gave his only Son, that whoever believes in him should not perish but have eternal life."
—John 3:16

"God loves each of us as if there were only one of us."
—St. Augustine

3

Exploring God's Love for You

Understanding, accepting, and believing how much God loves you helps create a solid foundation for your coaching sessions. Although you may have a healthy understanding of God's love, you may have doubted His love at some point in your life. These feelings of doubt can occur when you are experiencing problems in your life or when things don't happen in your life as planned. Delays and failures can cause anyone to be unhappy, but this unhappiness may cause you to doubt God's love. Regardless of your past experiences or disappointments, it's important you establish in your own heart and mind how much God loves you. It is this firm, unshakable revelation of God's love that can propel you to the place you want to be in life.

From personal experience, I have found that in order to overcome feelings of doubt, I must remain confident in God's love by focusing on what He has already done for me through His son Jesus. When I shift my thinking, I begin to realize there is no area of my life that God is not concerned about. Because He loves me so much, He cares about even the smallest details of my life. Recognizing His constant love for me not only floods my heart with peace but also helps me gain a greater perspective during stressful times.

When you read God's Word and begin to understand the depth of His love, it becomes easy to yield yourself completely to

Him. As you meditate and confess scriptures on God's love, you will become secure in His love for you. If you will take time to soak in the reality of this divine love, your emotions will begin to relax, your stress level will decrease, and your heart will be at peace—even during times of failure and delay!

Moreover, being rooted and grounded in God's love will provide the foundation for a successful coaching session. The work you do with your life coach is based on the belief that you are whole and complete. If you are a Christian, you have the Spirit of God living inside you, and He has already deposited the answers you need into your spirit. In Christ Jesus, you *are* a whole and complete person!

This truth reminds me of the Hebrew word, *shalom*, which refers to wholeness and completeness in every area of a person's life with nothing missing or incomplete. This term is also used when greeting or departing from someone. This completeness is found in Christ and our righteousness in Him.

When we doubt God's love for us and do not attempt to do anything to change our negative thoughts, we will not live up to our full potential in Christ. Eve, for example, doubted God's love for her in the Garden of Eden. Rather than running to God when she doubted His love for her, she turned away from Him. Her subsequent actions not only got her into trouble but also negatively impacted the entire human race.

It is crucial you remember that God is love and that His love for you is unchanging and self-sacrificing. As a child of God, there is nothing you can do to separate yourself from His love (Romans 8:38-39). No matter what has happened to you in the past, you can move forward towards your future confident of God's unfailing love for you!

Coach Application: Be supportive of your clients without judging them.

Client Application: Meditate on Psalms 119:1-18.

Reflection: How will you remain focused on God's love as you work with your coach, complete the assignments, and implement change? What measures can you put in place to keep you focused?

"Therefore, preparing your minds for action, and being sober-minded, set your hope fully on the grace that will be brought to you at the revelation of Jesus Christ."
−1 Peter 1:13 (ESV)

"Every man can, if he so desires, become the sculptor of his own brain."
–Santiago Ramon y Cajal

4

Neuroscience and the Bible

In *The Brain that Changes Itself*, Norman Doidge, M.D. writes, "The idea that the brain can change its own structure and functions through thought and activity is the most important alteration in our view of the brain since we first sketched out its basic component, the neuron."

In the most basic terms, neuroscience is the study of how energy moves through the brain. Neuroscientists have discovered that it is possible for new neural pathways to form in response to brain enrichment. The brain can change for the better, which means that it is possible to change the physical brain.

God has given us everything we need to live a victorious life. He has equipped us with the ability to renew our minds and establish healthy relationships. One way this can be accomplished is through what the scientific world refers to as "neuroplasticity." This refers to the human brain's remarkable capacity to form new neural connections throughout a person's life. As the brain responds to various thoughts, actions, and other stimuli, it makes neuron connections that create new pathways inside the brain.

I believe neuroscience research confirms our ability to use our brains to transform and renew our minds as instructed by God. Neuroscience also provides excellent examples of how fearfully and wonderfully we are created in the image of Christ. Through neuroscience, we are able to gain valuable knowledge from the Creator's immeasurable supply of knowledge.

The connection between neuroscience and Christianity is so important that Biola University's Center for Christianity regularly dictates time, money, and other resources to provide a platform to study the connection between neuroscience and Christianity. One such platform is "Neuroscience and the Soul," which explores the relationship between contemporary neuroscience and Christian belief.

God's written Word is full of powerful, positive confessions that, when believed on and acted upon in faith, have the ability to transform lives. This concept is not foreign to many coaching practices or neuroscience. Coaches who use positive coaching practices instead of negative ones are able to help clients uncover their hidden potential and take action. In fact, a study in *Social Neuroscience* tested the outcomes of several MRI examinations and found that optimistic coaching caused the brains of the participants to respond positively.

Although science is just now discovering principles of positive thinking, God has revealed this spiritual principle long ago in His Word. He knew how our brains are wired because He created them to function and respond to His Word. And the more we fill our minds with the truth from God's Word, the more our brains will begin to respond to that truth!

Coach Application: Keep in mind that science does not have the final authority, but it is a way by which we can glorify God. As you work with your client, don't become over-concerned with the science behind your coaching that you fail to acknowledge the Holy Spirit's work.

Client Application: Remember that science is subservient to God. Although science often reveals the principles of creation, it does not override the inherent authority found in Scripture.

Reflection: In many ways, the findings in neuroscience confirm what God says about the brain's ability to change. How can you use these findings to help you fully understand and activate the brain's power to respond to God's Word?

"Casting down imaginations, and every high thing that exalteth itself against the knowledge of God, and bringing into captivity every thought to the obedience of Christ." –2 Corinthians 10:5

"Your beliefs become your thoughts, Your thoughts become your words, Your words become your actions, Your actions become your habits, Your habits become your values,
Your values become your destiny."
—Mahatma Gandhi

5

Establishing Your Values

Values are those things in life that are important to you. Your upbringing, personal experiences, political and social culture, and religious beliefs can shape your values. As you work with your coach, he or she may ask that you share your values in order to gain insight or to help you remain on track towards your goals. As a Christian, some of your values might include:

- Submission to God (Mark 12:28-30)
- Love and respect for others (Mark 12:31)
- Humility (Philippians 2:2-8)
- Honesty and integrity (Colossians 3:9)
- Financial integrity (Matthew 25:14-30)

From my experience as a life coach and a coaching client, I believe that coaching sessions work best when we are able to determine and articulate our values. In most cases, we all come to the table with some pre-established values. Regardless, a life coach should be willing and able to help us identify our values.

One exercise that might help you to identify your values is to recall a time in your life when you felt happy, proud, and fulfilled. After recalling that memory, write down the specifics of that moment. Next, start to look for common themes that emerge from those moments. Ask yourself questions like these:

- Whom were you with at the time?
- What were you doing?
- Why were you engaged in the activity?

As these patterns start to emerge and you are able connect them to a specific value, you can begin to prioritize them and align your goals and life plans with them. Some of you may discover values like achievement and hard work are important to you. Others may esteem values like balance, generosity, and community.

Having a clear understanding of what motivates you, makes you happy, or drives you will help you to establish clear goals in future coaching sessions. It will also help you to gain more from your coaching sessions.

Keep in mind that your values are not necessarily right or wrong and that they may change over time. The more you uncover about yourself, the more you are able to identify your values and establish life plans that support your values.

Coach Application: Recognize that some beliefs are deeply rooted and that resistance to change will occur. Your role is to be patient yet challenging in order to help your client take full advantage of what coaching has to offer.

Client Application: Acknowledge your beliefs and be willing to adjust those that conflict with the Word of God. Meditate on Matthew 13:58, and ask God to reveal to you any areas of unbelief that are limiting you from moving forward.

Reflection: How can you use your values to help you be successful?

"For nothing will be impossible with God." – *Luke 1:37 (ESV)*

*"Dream so big you will look like an idiot if God
does not step in to help."*
— *Sandi Krakowski*

6

Dream Big for God

We were created to dream. As children we are full of dreams with little or no reserve about sharing them with anyone who will listen. Unfortunately, when we grow into adulthood and experience failure and rejection, we become hesitant to dream and to share our dreams with others. However, that is not what God desires. He wants His children to dream mega-size dreams in high definition! He wants us to pull our dreams off the shelf, dust them off, and immerse them in faith-filled words and actions.

As you're reading this chapter, think about the dreams tucked away in your heart. What are your biggest dreams and desires? What dreams are so huge that you don't dare mention them to anyone?

I encourage you to reengage and take hold of even your biggest dreams. Why? Because God placed those dreams in your heart for a reason, and He wants you to take action. God needs you to take action and collaborate with Him. He is not going to force you to dream, nor is He going to override your resistance to act on your dream.

Sad as it might be, if you do not move into action, you may very well die without experiencing all that God has for you. However, that is not God's desire. He wants to help you realize the dream that He has placed inside of you. All you have to do is let

Him guide you regarding what steps you need to take next.

Working with a life coach will help you to release those God-given dreams inside you. Part of your plan when working with your coach is to recognize and eliminate distractions that keep you from moving forward with action.

I have found that many of my distractions are attached to some form of emotion that I am trying to avoid. Once I identify the emotion I am experiencing or trying to avoid, I can neutralize its power to negatively impact my life.

Here is the normal process I use when reengaging my dreams:

1. **I guard my dream and watch out for the dream slayers.** I'm sure you're familiar with dream slayers in your life as well. They are the ones who are full of negativity and who are quick to share with you the many reasons why your dream will not come to pass.

2. **I feed my dream by speaking faith-filled promises found in the Word of God.**

3. **I pray about the direction I should take concerning my dream.**

4. **I resist the urge to limit my dreams to my abilities, knowledge, and wisdom.**

5. **I commit to accomplishing my dream no matter what obstacles I encounter.**

Some dreams God has placed in my heart are so huge that I am in awe at the very thought of them. One of my dreams is to expand Esteem House, a non-profit organization that I established, into a national program with centers across the United States and abroad. Esteem House was created to help educate teen girls on how to fulfill their God-given purpose in life. Its mission is to empower girls by teaching them the Word of God so they can become effective leaders among their peers and in their communities. Esteem House will provide these young women with a solid foundation for a personal relationship with Christ Jesus and for personal development, positive life skills, family wellness, financial literacy, and career development.

At one time, I had placed this dream on the back shelf where it collected cobwebs and multiple layers of dust. However, as I worked with my life coach, she helped me to reengage this dream and move towards turning the dream into a reality. The dream is alive and active in my life, and I have learned how to remain focused on the dream and not the obstacles. Even when things appear to be at a standstill, I find a way to accomplish something that brings me closer to the manifestation of my dream. The dream of Esteem House being an international program that changes the lives of millions of girls across the country has not fully manifested, but it is no less real in my heart and in my mind.

Like me and my dream for Esteem House, many of you have big dreams in your hearts waiting to be birthed. I encourage you to seek the Lord regarding these dreams, pray about them, and begin putting your hand to them. As you dream big for God, He will equip you to bring about His dreams in you!

Coach Application: Meditate on Ephesians chapter 1. Note what God has done for you, in you, and through you in Christ Jesus. Ask Him to show you how to reveal those truths to your client in your next session.

Client Application: Meditate on Ephesians chapter 1. Note what God has done for you, in you, and through you in Christ Jesus. How does this revelation knowledge help you in moving towards your dreams?

Reflection: What dream have you put on hold? Why did you put it on hold? How can you work towards making it come true?

"Write the vision, and make it plain upon tables,
that he may run that readeth it."
—Habakkuk 2:2

"To accomplish great things, we must not only act, but also dream,
not only plan, but also believe."
-Anatole France

7

Becoming a Person of Vision

Having vision is the ability to see what others don't see. Vision provides direction, creates life, gives purpose, ignites passion, and fuels drive. Vision gives you the courage to continue and not give up. It will override disappointment and discouragement in times of doubt and uncertainty. It is a sustaining force of life that will help you develop a Christ-centered mindset.

Vision starts in the heart and is fueled by faith. God places vision within us. However, it is our responsibility to develop, feed, and nurture it. Without vision, we will lead an unfulfilling life and perish without seeing the vision materialize. We can ignite our spirit by expanding our vision.

In order to become a person of vision, you must first focus on the greatness and goodness of God. One of the greatest demonstrations of God bringing forth vision in a man's heart is found in Genesis 13:14-17: *"The Lord said to Abram, 'Look as far as you can see in every direction—north and south, east and west. I am giving all this land, as far as you can see, to you and your descendants as a permanent possession. And I will give you so many descendants that, like the dust of the earth, they cannot be counted! Go and walk through the land in every direction, for I am giving it to you.'"*

In this passage, God places a vision inside of Abram regarding how expansive his offspring would become. Abram might not have fully understood the vision God had for him, but he accepted and acted upon it.

When God places a vision in your heart, He desires this same thing of you as He did of Abraham. Once you take hold of the vision, you must feed it with the Word of God by speaking scripture-based affirmations over yourself and your vision. The vision may appear too large to comprehend, but if God spoke something to your heart, then receive it, believe it, and act upon it. Dare to be a person of vision!

Coach Application: Your role is to understand that being a person of vision may not come naturally to your client. This may require constant clarification to confirm your understanding of the client's vision. When doing so, be certain not to lead the client. Allow him or her to locate, specify, and communicate that vision to you.

Client Application: To help uncover or sharpen your vision, spend time purposefully daydreaming about your future. Journal your thoughts and ideas. What do you see yourself doing in five years? What specific dreams and goals are in your heart? Now is a time to think big about your future!

Reflection: Is your vision limited by your fear? If so, how can you move past the fear?

"And since we have the same spirit of faith, according to what is written, 'I believed and therefore I spoke,'
'we also believe and therefore speak."
—2 Corinthians 4:13

"Refuse to criticize, condemn, or complain. Instead, think and talk only about the things you really want."
—Brian Tracy

8

Positive Affirmations

When creating or choosing positive affirmations, it is good to know that God's Word is an infallible source for affirmation. God's Word is sealed with integrity and backed by the blood of Jesus. God is bound by His Word, and He is obligated by covenant to act on your behalf. God's Word will sustain you and cause you to prosper in your actions. It is so powerful that nothing can stand in your way when you use the Word in faith.

Furthermore, when you speak God's Word, you release God's supernatural power into your situation. Although you may not realize it, your words—whether good or bad—create and frame your world. Rather than speaking words of doubt, fear, and failure, use God's Word to create affirmations that generate the divine power of God in your life. As you do, you will experience God's best for you.

Speaking affirmations using the Word of God is not a natural act. You must train yourself to learn how to be an imitator of Christ by letting your conversations be in line with God's Word. You must continually speak the solution instead of your current circumstances. The spoken Word of God will defeat the attacks of the enemy. Moreover, the words you speak are an energy force that brings life and peace to your family, your surroundings, your emotions, and your relationships.

Below are some positive affirmations that can help change your life. Many of these are based on God's Word and can help you overcome any negative opinions you may have about yourself, your abilities, or your future. I encourage you to speak these over yourself every day!

- I am filled with God's light, love, and peace.
- I treat myself with kindness and respect.
- I don't have to be perfect; I just have to be me.
- I give myself permission to shine.
- I honor the gifts God has given me, and I share them with others.
- I'm proud of all I have accomplished in Christ Jesus.
- I am greater than my fears.
- I love myself.
- I am my own best friend and cheerleader.
- Thank you Lord for the qualities, traits, and talents that make me so unique.
- The creative power of God is working in my life.
- I have loving thoughts towards others.
- I graciously give and receive God's love.
- People seek me out to bless me.
- God's best is available to me and I receive it now.
- God is the Master of my life.
- I am a distribution center of God's love and prosperity.
- All things are working in harmony causing good to come into my life.
- My value is priceless.

Please note that engaging in affirmations alone without faith in God's ability to create a change in you will not result in success. In order for positive affirmations to produce results in your life, you must combine them with faith in God's Word and follow them up with action.

Coach Application: Meditate on Philippians 4:8. Encourage your clients to stay focused on positive thoughts and words.

Client Application: Meditate on Philippians 4:8. Are you staying focused on positive words and thoughts?

Reflection: What can you do today to make sure you are speaking words that affirm your goals?

"He performs wonders that cannot be fathomed,
miracles that cannot be counted."
—Job 5:9

"I am the way, the truth, and the life. No one comes to the Father except
through Me."
—Jesus

9

Who Is God?

Allowing God to have the lead role in our lives and in our coaching sessions is crucial to our success. He is the source of truth, and we cannot find truth outside of the Spirit of Truth, which comes from God.

Although we are made in the image of God, we cannot afford to be deceived into thinking that we are God. Furthermore, we need to be aware of those who call themselves "Christians" but who believe there are many ways to God.

In 2 Timothy 3:1-9, Paul warned of people falling into grave deception in the last days: *"But mark this: There will be terrible times in the last days. People will be lovers of themselves, lovers of money, boastful, proud, abusive, disobedient to their parents, ungrateful, unholy, without love, unforgiving, slanderous, without self-control, brutal, not lovers of the good, treacherous, rash, conceited, lovers of pleasure rather than lovers of God—having a form of godliness but denying its power. Have nothing to do with such people. They are the kind who worm their way into homes and gain control over gullible women, who are loaded down with sins and are swayed by all kinds of evil desires, always learning but never able to come to a knowledge of the truth. Just as Jannes and Jambres opposed Moses, so also these teachers oppose the truth. They are men of depraved minds, who, as far as the faith is concerned, are rejected. But they will not get very far because, as in the case of those men, their folly will be clear to everyone"* (NIV).

As you work towards your personal life goals, it's crucial to remember that without God, you can't succeed on your own. You need His help, His wisdom, His Word, and His direction in your life. Regardless of how gifted or talented you may be, remember that without the grace of God, you would be destitute in your sin. Above all else, remember to first acknowledge God's presence, power, and ability in your life. Be humble before Him, and allow Him to lead and promote you.

Coach Application: Continue to create an atmosphere of trust and transparency in your sessions. Beware of using your sessions as an avenue of criticism or judgment.

Client Application: Ask God to reveal Himself to you. Be willing to spend some time in silence and expectation as you wait for God to reveal His love to you.

Reflection: How does understanding who God is from the Scriptures impact your actions, thoughts, and decisions? Is your idea of God the same as reflected in the Bible? If not, why? What are you going to do about your impression of God? (Read the following scriptures for further study: 1 John 4:8; 2 Peter 3:9; John 14:6; Isaiah 40:28; Psalm 18:30; 1 John 4:14; Isaiah 41:10; John 14:17; John 17:3.)

"But when the Helper comes, whom I shall send to you from the Father, the Spirit of truth who proceeds from the Father, He will testify of Me."
–John 15:26 (NKJV)

"Search well and be wise, nor believe that self-willed pride will ever be better than good counsel."
–Aeschylus

10

The Holy Spirit: The Ultimate Life Coach

The Holy Spirit can help guide you through any challenge or growth area in life. The purpose of the Holy Spirit is to help Christians transform into God's goodness. He will also empower you to bear witness of Jesus. Equally important, He will guide you by an inward witness in your spirit.

The Holy Spirit is part of the divine trinity, which includes the Father, the Son and the Holy Spirit. In John 14:16 Jesus refers to the Holy Spirit as the Comforter who will remain with a believer forever. In fact, the Amplified expounds the definition of *Comforter* to include the words *Counselor*, *Helper*, *Intercessor*, *Advocate*, *Strengthener*, and *Standby*.

The role of the Holy Spirit is vital in helping you to establish or renew your confidence in Christ. The Holy Spirit can provide you with the insight and strength you need to make lasting changes in your life.

The Holy Spirit produces peace and brings supernatural counsel and help when you need it. As a child of God, you can put yourself in a position to hear His voice by walking in love and spending time in God's Word.

Although it's wonderful to seek help and wisdom from family, friends, mentors, and life coaches, no one person can replace the divine wisdom that comes from the Holy Spirit. His wisdom is perfect, and He has all the answers you need. So as you're pursuing counsel from a life coach, don't forget to seek counsel from the Holy Spirit. He is the ultimate life coach!

Coach Application: As a coach, it's important for you to remember that you are not God. However, you have access to God through Jesus to receive guidance by the Holy Spirit.

Client Application: Although your coach is only human, he or she can help you work through obstacles and overcome setbacks.

> **Reflection:** How can you begin to incorporate the Holy Spirit into your coaching sessions and everyday life?

"The Lord is my strength and my shield; in him my heart trusts, and I am helped; my heart exults, and with my song I give thanks to him."
–Psalm 28:7 (ESV)

"The flesh, or human nature, is generally lazy and self-centered."
–Joyce Meyer

11

Christ-Centered or Self-Centered

You set the highest standard for your coaching sessions when you establish that Jesus is the only path leading to God and that your true identity is found in Him. Any attempt to find your true identity outside of Christ will promote self-centeredness, and any gain you achieve will be temporary.

As you begin to experience success in your coaching sessions, it is important to maintain a Christ-centered mindset. This will help keep you grounded in Christ while minimizing the chances of becoming self-centered. You can remain Christ-centered by focusing on who you are in Christ and by allowing the Holy Spirit to guide you into all truth.

Developing a mindset for success begins by establishing a relationship with Jesus Christ as your Lord and Savior. The more you study, meditate, and obey God's Word, the more you will understand who God is and who He is in you. As you grow in your walk with the Lord by feeding on the Word and fellowshipping with Him, you will begin to reflect Christ-likeness in your attitudes and behavior. Becoming Christ-centered in all you say and do is one of the greatest keys to long-term success you will ever find!

Coach Application: Engage your clients in exploratory dialogue to help them uncover areas of their lives where they find themselves fighting to have the last word or needing to always be right at all cost. Then ask them to consider the motive behind their actions.

Client Application: Ask God to reveal to you how you can focus on being like Him and achieving His desires for your life.

Reflection: What areas of your life are driven by selfishness? How can you change them to become more Christ-centered?

"Do not conform to the pattern of this world, but be transformed by the renewing of your mind. Then you will be able to test and approve what God's will is—his good, pleasing and perfect will."
—Romans 12:2 (NIV)

"It takes but one positive thought when given a chance to survive and thrive to overpower an entire army of negative thoughts."
—Robert H. Schuller

12

The Power of Your Thoughts

No one likes to waste money, but that is what you will be doing if you hire a coach and don't take responsibility for controlling your thoughts. Your coach's role is to help you work through your thoughts, but he or she cannot control your thoughts. You alone are held responsible for your thought life.

Your thoughts have tremendous power. They frame your words and actions and, thereby, create the life you live. The life you are experiencing today is a result of positive and negative thoughts. Negative thoughts not confronted and dealt with will create frustration and disappointment.

Thankfully, there is good news! *You* have the power to implement changes in your thought life that will bring about positive transformation. You do not have to continue on your current path of unfulfilled goals and buried dreams. God is ready and willing to help you be an agent for the change you want to experience in your life.

While you cannot necessarily control all of the external occurrences in your life, you have the authority to control the internal dialogue taking place in your mind. As you renew your mind and rid it of all of the toxic sludge that has accumulated over the past, you will begin to experience positive change.

The Bible is full of scriptures on how to renew your mind

to the Word of God. When you meditate on these scriptures and act upon them, they will become real in your life. Because God loves you so much, He has also provided instructions to help guide your thought life. One of these instructions or guides can be found in Philippians 4:8: "*And now, dear brothers and sisters, one final thing. Fix your thoughts on what is true, and honorable, and right, and pure, and lovely, and admirable. Think about things that are excellent and worthy of praise*" (NLT).

There are many other scriptures found in the Bible teaching us about our thoughts and beliefs. These scriptures tell us how to change our minds and show us the benefits and consequences of our thought life. For example, Proverbs 23:7 tells us that our thoughts create who we are. Philippians 4:8 describes the types of thoughts we should dwell upon. And 2 Corinthians 10:5 instructs us to cast down thoughts that are contrary to Christ. By acting upon these scriptures and thinking in line with God's Word, we can improve the quality of our lives and futures.

Our thoughts, beliefs, and behaviors are all intertwined with each other. Each of these create an energy force that has a huge impact on the quality of life we live. This energy force is so powerful that it surrounds us and determines how we view ourselves and how others view us.

We must remember that entertaining negative thoughts is like walking around in quicksand. The more we entertain these negative thoughts, the deeper we sink—until at some point we become immobile.

Like many of you, I've struggled with overcoming negative thoughts. I remember one time in particular when my husband and I were on vacation in Hawaii visiting with friends. While enjoying the beach and sun, I suddenly got this strong urge to write. At first, I did not know what to write or why the urge had become so strong. During my prayer time, I asked the Lord to reveal to me where this urge had come from. He said that it was always His intention for me to become a writer. However, my lack of confidence in His ability to create a good work in me had held me back from receiving.

He then reminded me of an incident in high school with an English teacher who ridiculed me about my writing. At the time, I had worked so hard on my assignments but continued to receive an average or below-average grade. I began to think that no matter how hard I worked on my writing, all the results would be the same. Unfortunately, this faulty line of thinking had stayed with me all through college and graduate school.

As I sat at the dining room table in Hawaii, God reminded me that I had been delivered from that faulty thinking and that it was time to move ahead with what He wanted me to do in the area of writing. To my surprise, I began writing and writing and writing.

Later one morning, I woke up with negative thoughts beginning to pound my brain: *What if no one likes what I write? What if my writing is not good enough?* But something was different about that morning. As the negative thoughts began to arise in my mind, I counteracted them by speaking positive truths from God's Word. I was finally able to push through the barrier that had kept me from moving forward in my writing. I let go of the need to be perfect in myself and began to rely on God's perfection.

While on vacation, I challenged myself to write something every day. I made a conscious decision not to judge my writing but to focus more on the freedom of expression. Since then, I have written over fifty blog posts and more than twenty articles. Had I not confronted my fear and self-doubts head-on, I would not have been able to progress in my writing.

Regardless of what fears, insecurities, and doubts may be plaguing your mind, refuse to give in to them. Instead, fill your heart with truths from God's Word and target your mind on positive, faith-filled thoughts. As you take control of your thoughts, you will take control of your life and your future!

Coach Application: Be on the lookout for any signs that may reveal some of your clients' inner fears or self-doubts. Take note of their patterns in behavior, voice, and expression. When you discover certain fears or doubts, encourage your clients to confront them with positive confessions from God's Word.

Client Application: Challenge yourself to track your thoughts throughout your day. What do you tend to think about while driving to work or waiting in line? Note these thought patterns and confront any negative thoughts or doubts with positive confessions from God's Word.

Reflection: What specific thoughts might be holding you back from moving forward? Address these with your coach.

"So God created man in his own image, in the image of God he created him; male and female he created them."
–Genesis 1:27 (ESV)

"If you put yourself in a position where you have to stretch outside your comfort zone, then you are forced to expand your consciousness."
−Les Brown

13

Discovering the True You

During your coaching sessions, your coach might use the terms *true self* and *false self*. The *true self* in coaching circles refers to who you are when you are living to your full potential; your *false self* is the behavior represented when you begin to engage in doubt and negative self-talk.

To help you distinguish between your true self and false self, it might be helpful to view your true self as the person God created you to be—who you are in Christ Jesus. The image of the false self is based on carnal thoughts and the lies of the devil. Your false self can be very powerful, but the power of God's Word used in faith is more powerful. However, you must be willing to investigate when and how your false self is formed, and you must be willing to do the work required to take back the power.

Your true self begins with cultivating a Christ-centered mindset. This way of thinking starts and ends with the Word of God.

Listed below are twenty-four principles that will help you release your false self and embrace your true self. I encourage you to think about these principles, meditate on the scriptures given, and apply these steps to your coaching sessions. I trust these will help you tremendously as you move forward in accomplishing your dreams and goals.

Positive change starts with accepting help from God.
Read and study the following scriptures:

Ephesians 2:8-10	Isaiah 43:18-19	Joel 2:12-13
John 10:10	2 Corinthians 5:1	Romans 12:2
Matthew 18:3		

The Holy Spirit is the ultimate life coach.
Review Jeremiah 29:11-15 and John 14:6.

The power you need to experience and sustain change is found in Christ.
See the following scriptures:

James 1:17	Isaiah 40:31	Numbers 23:19
Philippians 3:21	Hebrews 13:8	

Engage in faith-filled prayer prior to and during your coaching session.
Read these passages:

Mark 11:24	James 1:5	Philippians 4:6-7
1 John 5:14-15		

Meditate on the Word of God and make it the final authority in everything you do.
Study 2 Timothy 3:16-17.

Use Word-based affirmations.
Word-based affirmations provide God with a starting point to create change on your behalf.

Establish your joy in Christ.
Review the following passages:

Proverbs 17:22	Psalm 32:11	Psalm 28:7
Job 8:21	Psalm 16:11	

Make forgiveness a priority.
Meditate on Luke 6:37.

Understand that obedience is the will of God.
Read Romans 6:16 and John 14:15.

Seek God when determining which coach is best for you.
Study 1 John 4:1 and Psalm 1:1-6.

Let faith be the carrier of the change you want to experience.
Review Galatians 2:20.

Act on the Word—not on emotions and theory.
Read James 1:4 and Luke 6:3-35.

Remain focused.
See Isaiah 50:7, Proverbs 16:3, and Matthew 24:13.

Establish and maintain your identity in Christ.
Read 2 Corinthians 5:17 and John 15:5.

Trust God to create in you a lasting change.
Study Proverbs 3:5, Hebrews 11:1, and Psalm 28:7.

Create a written plan and mental vision of the result you desire.
Review Proverbs 29:18 and Habakkuk 2:2.

Resist rejection and avoid offense.
Meditate on Proverbs 19:11, Ecclesiastes 7:21-22, and Leviticus 19:18.

Monitor the internal dialogue in your head, and plant positive thought seeds.
See Romans 12:2.

Conquer intimidation and fear.
Read Isaiah 41:10.

Walk in the spirit of love.
Review Galatians 5:16-25.

Leave the past behind.
You cannot change your past, but you can change your perspective. During your coaching sessions, you might be asked to revisit past occurrences both good and bad. When doing this, keep in mind that Christ has healed you from any negative events. He has restored you and made you whole. It is your responsibility to walk in the provision provided by God. Your past contains no power to defeat you unless you reject the power given to you through Christ Jesus. As you revisit the negative occurrences contributing to your negative and faulty thinking, remember that Christ has made you a new creature!

Review the following passages:

2 Corinthians 5:17	Ephesians 2:10	Romans 8:1
1 Peter 1:23	John 5:4	1 John 4:4

Maintain a clean and pure heart.
See these scriptures:

Luke 5:4-5	1 Timothy 1:5	Matthew 5:8
2 Timothy 2:22	Ezekiel 36:26	Psalm 51:10

Receive and walk in your righteousness.
Review the following passages:

1 John 3:7	Genesis 15:6	Philippians 3:9
Romans 3:22	Ephesians 2:8-10	2 Corinthians 5:21
Galatians 2:20	Romans 8:1-39	

Expect the blessings of God to manifest in your life.
Meditate on James 1:17, Philippians 2:13, 3 John 1:2, and Numbers 6:24-26.

Coach Application: Champion your clients and acknowledge their accomplishments. Even individuals who seem confident and assertive still need encouragement from you.

Client Application: Write three to five positive affirmations on sticky notes and place them around your home or office. As you see these notes throughout your day, read them out loud and reflect on them.

Reflection: What keeps you from being whom God created you to be? What is the one thing you can do today to make a change? Share this with your coach and ask him or her to help you devise a plan of action.

"That I might make thee know the certainty of the words of truth; that thou mightest answer the words of truth to them that send unto thee."
−Proverbs 22:21

"The quality of our lives depends not on whether or not we have conflicts, but on how we respond to them."
−Tom Crum

14

How to Handle Conflicting Information

During your coaching sessions, your coach may present something that does not line up with your spiritual beliefs or appears to deviate from your overall mission. Instead of letting the matter fall by the side, it is best to address the matter immediately rather than allowing it to possibly deteriorate the relationship. Your coach is a professional who has your best interests at heart, and he or she will respect your honesty and transparency.

Let me give you an example of this from my own life. When I was working on a life coach course, I struggled with some material that was being presented and began to wonder if I was making the right decision. I voiced my concerns with the facilitator. She expressed her point of view concerning the matter, and while I disagreed, I asked the Lord for guidance.

Shortly thereafter, one day in my prayer time, the Lord reminded me of a time when I was attending a workshop at church. On the last day of the workshop, the speaker said something that was contrary to the Bible. As we all sat there, our "spiritual antennas" went on full alert.

The following Sunday during our normal church service, our pastor corrected what had been taught in error the prior week. He closed the matter by telling us that ninety-nine percent of what we heard was good information and supported by Biblical principles. His last statement was, "Don't throw the baby out with the bath water." While I am not a fan of that saying, I understood the meaning.

Similarly, when you disagree with something that your coach shares or suggests, take time to judge it against the Word of God. If it contradicts what's in the Bible, simply throw it out. Receive the good, but reject the bad. That's a pretty simple way to navigate through any questionable life coaching experiences you may have!

Coach Application: Respect your client's right to disagree. Establish guidelines for handling conflict before any conflict occurs.

Client Application: Maintain a cautious perspective, and pick your battles with care. Know when to confront and when to retreat.

Reflection: When you are faced with conflict, the resolution you need begins with you. Take a good look in the mirror, and be brutally honest about what you see and feel. Allow your heart, mind, and spirit to welcome the opportunity to learn from this experience and grow into a stronger person. Read the following scriptures and take a few minutes to write about how you can apply them to your current situation: Romans 5:2-5, 1 Corinthians 10:13, Matthews 18:15-17, and Colossians 3:13.

"Don't repay evil for evil. Don't retaliate with insults when people insult you. Instead, pay them back with a blessing. That is what God has called you to do, and he will bless you for it."
—*1 Peter 3:9 (NLT)*

"Our response to an offense determines our future...
A person who cannot forgive has forgotten how great
a debt God has forgiven them."
—*John Bevere*

15

Unforgiveness

Living your life with unforgiveness is like taking poison and expecting the other person to die. It can also hinder you from getting the most out of your coaching sessions. The act of forgiving is not for the benefit of the person who offended or hurt you; it's for your benefit! Forgiveness liberates you and moves you forward to what God has for you.

For some, forgiveness is immediate. For others, forgiveness might be a daily occurrence for the same offense. For most, it comes with revelation and over time.

The power of forgiveness is not only spiritual but physical as well. A study conducted by Charlotte vanOyen Witvliet, a psychologist at Hope College, revealed that when people recalled a feeling of resentment, they became physically stimulated. They experienced an increase in both their blood pressure and heart rate. However, when Witvliet instructed the participants to have compassion towards their offenders or to visualize forgiving them, they experienced positive reactions. (Information taken from http://greatergood.berkeley.edu/article/item/the_new_science_of_forgiveness.)

Like many of you, I've had many opportunities to forgive those who have hurt me in the past. I remember one instance in particular that happened a few years ago. My family had brought a certain person into our home to be a part of our family, but this individual ended up betraying me. I grieved the loss of the friendship, and my heart grew harder every day towards that person because of what had been done to my family and me.

As the years went by, people who came into my life paid the price in some way or another for the actions of that one person. Many years after the incident, I attempted to reconcile the relationship but failed. As I look back, I realize I didn't want to reinstate the relationship; I simply wanted to erase the rejection I felt. However, that was not possible.

Finally, I knew I had held onto the hurt long enough. It was time for me to forgive and I did...again, again, and again...until I got so fed up with the process! I resolved that it was not going to happen, and I buried it deep inside.

While working with my coach, I was able to identify the reason why I was holding on to the pain and resentment. I finally realized that the anger was not towards that person; it was towards my parents. I was angry they could love and forgive this person and move forward. Because I had invited the Holy Spirit to guide me in my coaching sessions, I believe I was able to identify the root of my anger, forgive everyone involved, and move forward. I realized forgiveness was a choice, and I had made the choice to forgive.

Bernard Meltzer once said, "When you forgive, you in no way change the past—but you sure do change the future." The moment we choose to forgive those who have hurt us is the moment we liberate ourselves from the chains of unforgiveness. By forgiving the past hurts and pains, we embrace the possibility of a bright and glorious future.

Coach Application: Be on the lookout for instances of unforgiveness, and address them using International Coaching Federation Core Competencies such as active listening and powerful questioning. As you help the client uncover any areas of unforgiveness, refrain from judging him or her during this process. You may need to also avoid internal attunement by separating your personal issues and concerns and focusing solely on the client.

Client Application: Acknowledge how past experiences have influenced your ability to forgive others. Ask your coach to help you identify ways to resolve or deal with those internal triggers.

> **Reflection:** Are you holding resentment, unforgiveness, or animosity towards someone? If so, write down his or her name along with a brief description of the situation, and ask your coach to help you work towards resolution.

"Write the vision; make it plain on tablets,
so he may run who reads it."
– Habakkuk 2:2 (ESV)

"In the Psalms, David writes what he honestly feels. We should be
honest too, when we talk about our problems."
–Rick Warren

16

Journaling Your Way to Success

You might be tempted to ignore the benefits of journaling or dismiss them as a waste of time. However, I urge you not to give in to that temptation. Journaling is a key component to your success. According to a study from 2002 by Ochsner, Sner, Bunge, Gross, and Gabrieli, you can experience peace, release of pressure, and overall well-being when you associate written words with your emotions. In a 2000 study, Pennebaker revealed that, over time, journaling can lead to clarity and a reduction in stress.

When you first embark upon your journaling process, don't be surprised if you experience internal resistance, or if you find it to be tedious or boring–this is not unusual. The key is to start and stick to it! The process works. Yes, there will be times when you find you have nothing to write about. When this occurs, try writing about what you are feeling at the time. Don't be afraid to let loose. This is your personal journal for your eyes only. You are free to express yourself without fear or retaliation from anyone, including yourself.

As you allow your words to flow freely in your journal, you will find that you have much to write about during your designated journaling time. The key is to be committed to the process.

William Hutchinson Murray described the commitment

process this way: "Until one is committed, there is hesitancy, the chance to draw back. Concerning all acts of initiative (and creation), there is one elementary truth, the ignorance of which kills countless ideas and splendid plans: that the moment one definitely commits oneself, then Providence moves too. All sorts of things occur to help one that would never otherwise have occurred. A whole stream of events issues from the decision, raising in one's favor all manner of unforeseen incidents and meetings and material assistance, which no man could have dreamed would have come his way. Whatever you can do, or dream you can do, begin it. Boldness has genius, power, and magic in it. Begin it now."

Some of you may be quite adept at journal writing, others of you may have more trouble committing to the process. For those of you who are trying this for the first time, I'd like to encourage you from my own personal experience.

A few years ago, my life coach explained to me the significance of journaling and its connection to my success. Having never been a person who kept a diary as a child or as an adult, I was not fully vested in the process in the beginning. However, because I was committed to the process and trusted my coach's guidance, I agreed to do it. In fact, I was asked to sign a personal contract with myself stating that I would commit to journaling as a part of my own self-care.

As instructed, I reluctantly got up early the next morning to start my journaling. I made myself a cup of coffee, got distracted by the clutter on my desk, and ended up working on other projects. Obviously, my first attempt did not work out as planned!

About an hour into working, I remembered the advice my life coach had offered me. She had instructed me to start my journaling and meditation immediately upon waking up because that was when my emotions were more accessible.

By the time I had returned to my journal that first morning, everyone else in my home was up and moving around the house. All chance of finding a quite space was lost.

The next morning, I got up, grabbed my journal and pen, proceeded to my favorite chair, and snuggled in to begin the process. I was ready to begin my thirty minutes of self-care, which included twenty minutes of writing and ten minutes of reflection and gratitude. I started my time with prayer asking the Holy Spirit to reveal to me those things that needed to be revealed and released.

Once I finished, I stared out of the window, waiting on the rapid overflow of emotions to come racing out of me and onto the paper. It did not occur at first. As I watched out the window admiring the sunrise, I began to let my mind drift to the day's to-do-list. Regaining my focus, I forced myself to return to the task at hand. I began writing about having nothing to journal about, which led to writing about how I felt in regards to having nothing to write about. This finally led to the realization that maybe I did not have anything valuable to write. Then suddenly, bingo! I hit a gusher, and the words began to flow.

As I continued with regular journaling exercises, my writing became deeper and more revealing. Yes, there were days when I was dry, but I pushed through the barriers. I had come to learn that when I felt emotionally dry, there was something brewing in me that needed to be addressed.

It's possible some of you may have had similar experiences and breakthroughs with your journaling experiences. I encourage you to continue pressing on! Your consistent determination and effort will pay off in the end.

Coach Application: Help the client embrace journaling as part of the coaching process by explaining the benefits that can lead to self-discovery.

Client Application: Consider beginning your day with journaling. When you journal first thing in the morning, your mind is less cluttered. Writing by hand will help keep you free from distractions on your computer.

Reflection: What emotions are you internalizing? Consider releasing them through your writing. Remember, you are not being graded on your journal writing. Use your journaling as a time to express your internal thoughts and emotions.

"Call to me and I will answer you, and will tell you great and hidden things that you have not known."
–Jeremiah 33:3 (ESV)

"Prayer is where the action is."
–John Wesley

17

Prayer

You can fuel your coaching sessions with prayer. Prayer paves the way for change and revelation. When you are praying about your coaching sessions, be specific about what you want to see and experience. Find scriptures that support your desired outcome.

When you pray, stay in faith. Refuse to focus on the negative, and don't complain about how bad things are or why they will not change. This kind of focus in prayer will only depress you. Moreover, it does not give God anything to work with on your behalf. Besides, God does not want to hear about your self-described failures and shortcomings. He views you through the blood of Jesus as perfect in the image of Christ.

Instead, pray for the desired result and believe you receive the answers to your prayers. When doubt rises up, resist it as instructed in James 4:7 (NIV), *"Submit yourselves, then, to God. Resist the devil, and he will flee from you."* Your doubt is not from God–it's from the devil. God has given you the power in Christ to overcome every threat and attack of the enemy!

As I've progressed in my walk with God, I've grown in my understanding of prayer. Once upon a time, when I heard people talk about prayer, my brain would shut down, my eyes would roll to the back of my head, and my body would go numb. Okay, perhaps it was not that bad. However, I was in limbo-land concerning prayer. I was a born-again Christian living for Jesus, but I had no real idea of how to pray and get results.

As I began to study the Bible and read other books on the subject of prayer, the Holy Spirit began to teach me about the principles of prayer. I came to learn that praying was not about following a set of rules. It is simply having a conversation with God using His Word concerning the matter I am facing. I learned to pray, listen for God's response, and respond with either more prayer, action, or both. As I prayed to God, I was opening the door for Him to come into the situation I was praying about and begin working on my behalf. Many answers came with a sense of knowing or peace in my spirit. Other answers came with a particular scripture I found during my devotion time. And some answers were confirmed from someone I trusted such as my pastor as he spoke from the pulpit.

I also learned to keep my prayers simple. I prayed to my Heavenly Father in the name of Jesus and according to God's Word. I did not get hung up on how long I prayed or if I prayed standing or sitting. I came to realize that God was only concerned about my heart.

Consequently, I discovered that prayer is not limited to any certain regimented timeframe. I am free to pray at any time of the day or night. I can actually pray all day if I prefer. Prayer is a lifestyle. It is not something I have to do; it is something I choose to do.

You, too, can learn how to pray effectively and according to the Bible. You don't have to wonder if your prayers are heard or if they work; you can be certain God hears and answers your prayers if you pray in faith and according to His Word.

I've listed some Scriptures here to help you grow in your understanding of prayer. As you study these scriptures, meditate on them, and apply them to your life, you will discover how to pray more accurately and with more results.

- *"He made known to us the mystery of his will according to his good pleasure, which he purposed in Christ."* – Ephesians 1:9 (NIV)

- *"I pray that the eyes of your heart may be enlightened in order that you may know the hope to which he has called you, the riches of his glorious inheritance in his holy people."* –Ephesians 1:18 (NIV)

- *"Finally, be strong in the Lord and in his mighty power. Put on the full armor of God, so that you can take your stand against the devil's schemes. For our struggle is not against flesh and blood, but against the rulers, against the authorities, against the powers of this dark world and against the spiritual forces of evil in the heavenly realms. Therefore put on the full armor of God, so that when the day of evil comes, you may be able to stand your ground, and after you have done everything, to stand. Stand firm then, with the belt of truth buckled around your waist, with the breastplate of righteousness in place, and with your feet fitted with the readiness that comes from the gospel of peace. In addition to all this, take up the shield of faith, with which you can extinguish all the flaming arrows of the evil one. Take the helmet of salvation and the sword of the Spirit, which is the word of God. And pray in the Spirit on all occasions with all kinds of prayers and requests. With this in mind, be alert and always keep on praying for all the Lord's people."* –Ephesians 6:10-18 (NIV)

- *"But the fruit of the Spirit is love, joy, peace, forbearance, kindness, goodness, faithfulness, gentleness and self-control. Against such things there is no law."* –Galatians 5:22-23 (NIV)

Coach Application: Pray for your clients. Consider praying for their understanding as instructed in Ephesians 1:8.

Client Application: Pray that God will strengthen you and reveal to you His good and perfect will as instructed in Romans 12:1-2.

Reflection: What is holding you back from praying regularly? Carve out a designated time in your schedule to pray daily.

"For we are His workmanship, created in Christ Jesus for good works, which God prepared beforehand that we should walk in them."
–Ephesians 2:10 (NKJV)

"Jesus came to announce to us that identity based on success, popularity, and power is a false identity–an illusion! Loudly and clearly He says, 'You are not what the world makes you; but you are children of God.'"
–Henri M. Nouwen

18

Your Identity in Christ

As you pray and allow God's Word to come alive in your heart, your heart opens to experience a clear image of who you are in Christ. When you see yourself as He does, your faults, disappointments, failures, and shortcomings will become less visible. Your feelings will no longer be your motivating factor. The negative opinions and labels of others will lose their power to define you.

When you allow God to be the lead coach during your coaching sessions, you will gain access to everything you need to flourish. It does not matter who you are, what you have done, or where you find yourself. When you surrender to God and commit your life to Him, you instantly receive the authority to use the name of Jesus and the righteousness of Jesus to live the life God created you to live.

I know this might all sound too good to be true or impossible, but I know first-hand how life can be transformed by the power of God. Learning the truth of my identity in Christ totally changed me and the course of my life.

I gave my heart to Christ when I was just six years old. At the time, I was not clear about what that meant beyond not going to hell. My reasons for surrendering my life to Christ were based entirely on my desire to avoid dying and going to hell. I did not know about the benefits, freedom, and authority granted to me as a child of God. I continued my relationship with God under this misconception throughout my childhood, teen years, and young adult life. I was "saved," but I was uneducated as to what that really meant. Ultimately, I was miserable.

I lived my life according to a set of rules prominent in the denomination in which I was raised. These rules included such notions that girls could not wear pants, make-up was unacceptable, and earrings could not be any larger than the size of a quarter. Boys were off limits and secular music was of the devil. Above all, I was conditioned to believe that if I did not watch out, God was going to punish me if I did something wrong.

I spent most of my childhood and early adult life being terrified of God and what He might do to me. It was not until my late twenties that I came into the knowledge of who I really was in Christ. I began to understand that God was not mad at me. He loved me, and He was not out to get me. God was more concerned with my heart than what I was wearing. His overwhelming love for me was so much more than rules and regulations—it was about grace, redemption, unmerited favor, unconditional love, and support.

Years later, during one of my own coaching sessions with my life coach, I came to realize how my view of God had shaped my life. Unbeknown to me, this incorrect view of God's nature created some faulty thinking on my part, which affected how I viewed myself and treated others. For example, because I thought God was always trying to catch me making a mistake so He could punish me, I developed an insecurity to those in authority and remained silent and withdrawn in hopes that I would fly under the radar. As a result, I was often lonely and dissatisfied with life.

By the grace of God and the renewing of my mind, I overcame my insecurities as well as my need to be perfect in my own right. I now live my life in God's perfection and see myself as whom He created me to be. Yes, there are days when my faulty thinking tries to come into play, but I am now able to quickly identify the source and characteristics of my faulty thinking. Now I can stop these negative tendencies from influencing my life and decisions.

Similarly, you can also experience the freedom gained from understanding God's true nature. I encourage you to focus on the goodness of God, His eternal love for you, and His redemptive work in Christ. The more you realize God's great love towards you, the more you will flourish in life.

Coach Application: Allow your clients the freedom to explore their identity in Christ.

Client Application: Meditate on 1 Corinthians 6:19-20.

Reflection: What can you do daily to remind yourself of your value and identity in Christ? Spend time meditating on a scripture of your choice that brings you joy and peace. Ask God to make that scripture alive in you.

"For there is one God, and there is one mediator between God and men, the man Christ Jesus."
−*1 Timothy 2:5 (ESV)*

"Striving for perfection only leads to endless procrastination, and endless procrastination makes you perfect in one thing only: procrastinating."
—*Marianne Songbird*

19

Perfection in Christ

In the previous chapter I shared how my unhealthy need for perfection opened doors to faulty thinking. I'm grateful for the help of the Holy Spirit who led me into the truth of God's Word. I'm also thankful for my life coach who helped me uncover the driving force behind the need for unrealistic perfections. This discovery led to the most freeing moment in my life as I abandoned my need to be perfect. In doing so, I learned that by abandoning my quest for perfection, I could start living the life of my dreams.

I also learned that perfection is a distant cousin of procrastination. Neither perfection nor procrastination has any place in coaching sessions. The quest for perfection will either set a person up for failure or paralyze him with fear.

The need for perfection is also the excuse we give when we are not sure what to do. Saying that we are waiting on the "perfect whatever" is the same as deciding to wait until "hell freezes over" to pursue our dreams. Since hell will literally never freeze over, we will never literally have that perfect moment. Rather than waiting for the perfect moment when the moon and stars are aligned, we must simply prepare the best we can for each step we take.

Although taking steps in an imperfect time can be frightening, it's helpful to have a hand to encourage and guide you along in the process. That's one reason having a life coach can be so rewarding during major transition points in life.

Before committing to your coaching sessions, it's important for you to prepare your heart and mind for the task ahead. Ask the Holy Spirit to guide you and launch you out into the deep.

As you begin to develop a plan with your life coach to pursue your dreams, you will have to be transparent. Yes, there will be times when you feel vulnerable, but that is okay. The payoff is worth it!

No one lives his or her dream life without experiencing some level of failure and vulnerability. But you can begin to live your dreams! Tomorrow is coming, and there is no guarantee you will be around to experience it. So don't wait another day, hour, or second. Starting now, remove the word "perfect" and all of its derivatives from your vocabulary. Launch out into the deep, and live your dream life!

Remember, it's okay to make a mistake. There are few mistakes from which you cannot recover. Choose today not to be ruled by fear or procrastination. You were created for greatness, but it will never manifest if you don't take the first step. When you are tempted to draw back and wait for perfection, remember these words from The Nester: "It doesn't have to be perfect to be beautiful."

Coach Application: Be supportive and patient with your clients; understand they may be uncomfortable reflecting on or accepting their perfection in Christ.

Client Application: Remain open to hear from the Holy Spirit as He speaks to your heart concerning your identity in Christ.

Reflection: What areas of your life do you criticize the most? Ask God to reveal to you the root cause of your negative perception, and ask Him to help you see yourself the way He sees you.

"Be anxious for nothing, but in everything by prayer and supplication, with thanksgiving, let your requests be made known to God; and the peace of God, which surpasses all understanding, will guard your hearts and minds through Christ Jesus."
−Philippians 4:6-7 (NKJV)

"Progress is impossible without change, and those who cannot change their minds cannot change anything."
–George Bernard Shaw

20

Change

You can be certain that an opportunity for change will occur during your coaching sessions. If you are not changing, something is wrong. Change is required for growth. Without change, your life will be severely limited indeed.

The key to embracing change is realizing that when you are faced with change, you might respond with fear, resistance, or defiance. However, you can minimize the impact of your response by remembering that, even in the midst of change, you have options. It is up to you to determine what you are willing to give up in exchange for what you desire. Remember, growth cannot come without change.

One way to transition through change is to uncover options that work best for you and your situation. Once you identify your options, take action and remain committed to the process. Change won't always be easy, but with the right attitude, it can be much more enjoyable.

Like you, I've had many opportunities to change the course of my life. I remember one particular crossroad I faced awhile back when everything in my life seemed to be going good. My closest friends and family supported me with unconditional love, my career was on track, and I was living the American Dream. I had a house and I was traveling the country. Although my life seemed the picture of success, I was unsettled. Life was good, but it wasn't great.

One day as I sat in my living room watching the sun bask in the golden haze that filled the room, I realized it was time for change. I heard the Lord speak to me in my spirit. It was not an audible voice but a knowing. It was time to go to Bible school. While I knew it was God speaking to me, I was still hesitant. At first, I thought people like me don't attend Bible school. After I heard from God, however, my perspective quickly changed.

I had come to a point of decision. My life was at a crossroads, and I knew if I took the step of going to Bible school that my life would drastically change. I had allowed the good in my life to become great. Life was going so well that that I did not want to lose everything I had going for me. In fact, I had just purchased my home less than six months ago and had not even unpacked all the boxes. I wasn't quite ready for my successful world to be shaken just for the sake of going to Bible school.

As a result, I decided to obey God partially. Yes, I know that partial obedience is disobedience, but I attempted to do it just the same. Rather than go to the school God had directed me to attend, I decided to take a class online. Surely, God was not concerned with where I went just as long as I enrolled in Bible school!

I signed up for an online Bible school and was pushing forward in my partial obedience. Two weeks before the class was scheduled to start, I received notification that the course had been canceled with no reschedule date available. As I sat there staring at the words, I heard a small voice on the inside, "Are you going to obey Me or not? I told you to go to a specific school."

You would think by that point I would have been onboard with what God had told me to do. I must admit I gave it one last-ditch effort. I began to tell God all the reasons why I couldn't do what He wanted me to do. Who was going to buy my house? Where would I live until school started? How would I support myself once

I got to school? Would they even let me into Bible school?

I struggled with the decision for several weeks until I finally decided to honor God and do what He wanted me to do. I submitted my application and began making preparations for the move.

When I called my realtor, I was too embarrassed to tell her over the phone that I was selling my home. Instead, I just asked her to come over to the house. When she arrived, I was a nervous wreck. My stomach was churning as we moved past the pleasantries and sat down for business. Finally, I told her I was moving and going to Bible school to prepare for ministry. Once I acknowledged the decision I had made, relief washed over me. Despite the sea of unknowns, my heart was full of peace. I knew nothing good in my life could replace the great things God had destined for me.

Perhaps some of you may be at a critical point of decision in your life. Maybe your life is going one way, but God is asking you to take a step in a completely different direction. You may have a lot riding on your decision to obey God's instructions, and there may be some sacrifices you may have to make in order to fulfill God's plan. But rest assured, obedience is always the best choice! If you will take that step of faith to obey God and make the change He's asking of you, He will grace you during your transition. You don't have to be afraid of the unknown; God's presence and peace are yours as you obey Him in all that you do.

Coach Application: In order for your clients to experience change, they must gain insight, experience an emotional response, and take action. You can help them by holding them accountable and asking challenging questions during your coaching sessions. This will allow them to explore any underlying emotions or resistance that might be preventing them from changing.

Client Application: Once you have gained insight, don't be afraid to embrace the emotion that follows. This is a part of the process that will lead you to change. Be sure to process your thoughts and emotions prior to the change, during the transition, and after the change.

Reflection: When have you encountered times of change in your life? Were you successful in handling change? Why or why not?

Appendix

Affirmation Exercise

Affirmations provide emotional support and encouragement. They can also help you change your behavior and create a new belief system. In order for affirmations to be effective, they must be positive and consistent; they must also speak of desired results in the present tense.

As you create your affirmations, take inventory of your positive traits and work to incorporate them into your affirmations. If you are not sure where to start, consider what characteristics you will need to exhibit in order for your goals to come to pass. When creating and saying your affirmations, be deliberate and present in mind and spirit. Don't just rattle them off. Instead, think about them and visualize yourself in line with what you are saying. You might find it easier to focus on one area at a time.

Generally, you should say your affirmations multiple times throughout the day. However, if you find this overwhelming, begin speaking them once a day and work up to twice a day. The key is to start and be consistent.

Listed below are some affirmations to help you get started in your daily confessions.

Christ-Centered Identity
- My value is established in Christ (Ephesians 2:6).
- I am valuable because Jesus paid the price for me
  (1 Peter 1:18-19).
- I am valuable because God lives inside me
  (1 Corinthians 6:19-20).
- God has a purpose and plan for my life (Jeremiah 29:11).
- I am full of strength and dignity (Proverbs 31:25).
- God values and loves me (John 3:16).
- I have the boldness of God (Proverbs 28:1).
- I am accepted by God (Ephesians 1:6).
- God delights in me (Psalm 18:19).
- I am a vessel of honor (2 Timothy 15-21).
- I belong to God (Ephesians 2:19).

Vision
- I am a person with vision.
- I see God's vision for me.
- God created me to dream, invent, explore, and create.
- My vision expands daily.
- I make quality decisions.

Faith
- My faith is awake.
- My faith is alive.
- My faith is actively working.
- My faith is stronger every day.
- My faith is producing results.

Revelation and Wisdom
- I am saved by God's grace.
- God freely gives me His wisdom (James 1:5).
- I am free in Jesus (Acts 13:39).
- I am full of wisdom and knowledge (Romans 15:14).

- I am complete in Christ (Colossians 2:10).
- I believe I receive what I ask of God (1 John 5:14-15).
- I am equipped for success.
- God always causes me to win.
- I am knowledgeable and ready for all circumstances (John 16:13; John 14:6).

Relationships
- God's love is operating in me (1 Corinthians 3:8).
- I plant seeds of affection and love in those around me (Galatians 6:7).
- My life is full of divine connections.
- I am established in love (Ephesians 3:17).

Mental and Physical Healing
- The Holy Spirit strengthens me (Ephesians 3:16).
- I have the mind of Christ (Philippians 2:5).
- God's peace guards my mind (Philippians 4:7).
- I operate in power and love with a sound mind (2 Timothy 1:7).
- I am healed (1Peter 2:24).
- God's Word in me brings healing.
- I choose life (Proverbs 18:21).
- My health and soul are prosperous (3 John 1:2).
- God gives me long life (Psalms 91:15-16).
- I overcome obstacles and challenges (1 John 4:4).

Business and Career
- My business/career is victorious in Christ (1John 5:4).
- I have the mind of Christ and the ability to operate in His power.
- I am an heir to the promises of God (Galatians 3:29).
- I have the power of God operating in my business/career (2 Corinthians 4:7).

- Spiritual blessings are operating on my behalf
  (Ephesians 1:3).
- I have the ability to plan a successful career and business
  (Genesis 11:6).
- My ministering angels are working in my business and career
  right now.

Peace and Joy
- My heart is strengthened by God (Psalms 73:26).
- My life is full of praise.
- Peace is mine (Proverbs 3:1-2).
- I have peace in God (Romans 5:1).
- I live in God's grace (Romans 6:14).

Led by God
- I am led by the Spirit of God.
- I am a spirit being who is able to communicate with God.
- I am aware of the inward witness and respond accordingly.

About the Author

DeNeen K. Attard, a certified life coach, can help you overcome the obstacles that are preventing you from achieving your personal and professional goals. As president of Attard Coaching & Consulting, DeNeen has a keen ability to help you clarify complex issues and set achievable, measurable goals.

Perhaps DeNeen's most outstanding attribute is her Christian perspective. This perspective, combined with effective coaching techniques, can empower you to take specific steps to get unstuck, move forward, and attain your prize. She can help you remain focused and committed to your life's goals and vision.

DeNeen's quick wit illuminates the adversities universal to everyone and helps alleviate the stress that accompanies facing tough personal truths. With over fifteen years of proven experience, she understands the importance of cultivating personal relationships to achieve goals and can show you how to develop healthy relationships in your personal and professional life.

Attard earned her Life Coach certification from Gardner Institute, Southlake Texas. She holds an M.S. in Management from Indiana Wesleyan and a B.A. in Organizational Communication from Indiana University Northwest. She is also a graduate of Rhema Bible Training College and Therapon Institute.

To schedule a coaching session, speaking engagement, or to order additional books, write:

DeNeen K. Attard
15821 FM 529, Suite 229
Houston, Texas 77095

Email: Deneen@DeneenAttard.com
Website: www.DeNeenAttard.com
Facebook: DeNeenAttardLifeCoach
Twitter: @DeneenAttard

www.ingramcontent.com/pod-product-compliance
Lightning Source LLC
LaVergne TN
LVHW021525080426
835509LV00018B/2668